Picturing Historic

Person
County

Picturing Historic
Person
County

EDDIE TALBERT
AND EDITH GREY

PHOTOGRAPHY BY
JOHN W. MERRITT

Charleston   London

History
PRESS

Published by The History Press
Charleston, SC 29403
www.historypress.net

Copyright © 2007 by Eddie Talbert
All rights reserved

All images by John W. Merritt, courtesy of the author.

First published 2007

Manufactured in the United Kingdom

ISBN 978.1.59629.289.5

Library of Congress CIP data applied for.

Contents

Acknowledgements

I would like to acknowledge the following people, without whom this book would not have been possible:
My wife, Terri M. Talbert.
My mother-in-law, Edith Grey Merritt.
Mrs. Jean Davis Newell, Mr. Wayne Buchanan and Mr. Otis Stephens.

I would also like to thank everyone who provided information for this book.

Introduction

The photographs in this book are part of a collection of photographs that were taken by John Wesley Merritt, a lifetime resident of Roxboro, North Carolina. Mr. Merritt, who was born on August 29, 1916, became interested in photography as a young boy. His interest in photography continued throughout his life, up until his death on April 17, 1996.

Mr. Merritt's first camera was a Brownie box camera, which he bought at the young age of seven or eight with a silver dollar that was given to him by a family member. This marked the beginning of a hobby that would continue to grow throughout his entire lifetime. As a teenager he became interested in developing his own film and making his own prints. His first efforts at developing his own photography began in a makeshift darkroom that was located in a small area of a bathroom in his parents' home.

After finishing Roxboro High School he attended Oak Ridge Military Institute and the University of North Carolina at Chapel Hill, and his interest in photography continued to thrive. He always carried a camera with him and took pictures at every opportunity. By this time he had long surpassed the simplicity of the Brownie box camera and was using the more advanced 35mm cameras. In 1941 he was drafted into the army and developing and printing his own pictures had to be put on hold temporarily. However, he still carried a camera with him at all times, although there were limits to what he could photograph.

After his discharge from the army in 1945 he proceeded to expand his interest in photography in a much bigger and better way for his own enjoyment. Mr. Merritt was now employed by Roxboro Cotton Mill so weekends were the only time he had available for working in his darkroom, which was now a small area in the home he shared with his wife and children. He was called on from time to time to take pictures for groups, reunions, schools and weddings, among other things. He enjoyed doing that, but because of full-time employment his time was limited and he only charged enough to cover materials. Mostly, he liked 35mm cameras because they were easy to carry and used film capable of taking more photographs than the earlier cameras. He enjoyed enlarging his photographs as well and was able to do this with the use of the 35mm film.

His own personal interests included photographing many of the everyday places and scenes in and about Roxboro and Person County. This included schools, churches, hospitals, parades, public buildings, street scenes, farms and local sporting events. He also took a number of pictures inside the Roxboro Cotton Mill, Longhurst Cotton Mill and the Collins and Aikman plant. He made portraits upon request as well and photographed dance recitals and stage shows at the Palace Theater. Wherever things were happening, John Merritt was sure to be there with his camera.

Along came the introduction of color photography and people became more fascinated with this new concept. Subsequently, black-and-white photography was no longer in demand. Mr. Merritt never expanded his hobby to include the development of color photos because it was more complicated and he just didn't have the space in the small darkroom located in his home.

A large number of the photographs that John Merritt took were never printed until recently. These negatives were stored for safekeeping over the years and it wasn't until family members started looking through these negatives after Mr. Merritt's death that a newfound interest in his photography began to develop. The current interest was fueled by selecting a few negatives at a time to be printed. The more photos that were printed, the more the interest grew to have even more printed. Before long, a number of Person County residents began to express an interest in seeing more of Mr. Merritt's photography.

Roxboro has undergone many changes over the years, most of which would be forgotten if not for photographs. With the development of shopping centers and malls, Main Street is no longer the same. Schools have been torn down; churches have been expanded. Textile plants are gone and fewer farmers grow tobacco. Warehouses are no longer used for tobacco auctions and trains don't pass through town on a regular basis. There is no public transportation. Many of the buildings still standing have been remodeled.

The photographs in this book have been selected from the photos that Mr. Merritt took during the 1940s and 1950s. Most of the photographs were not intended to capture any special events, although parades were considered very special in a small town and the townsfolk turned out in large numbers for these occasions. Not only are these photographs representative of some of his best work, but they illustrate a period in the history of Roxboro and Person County. These are times that are gone forever but can be remembered and preserved through the photography that Mr. Merritt so diligently produced as he pursued and enjoyed a hobby that interested him for most of his life.

My interest in putting together a book of this nature grew from an exhibit of Mr. Merritt's photography held at the Kirby Art Gallery in August 2005. A display of about fifty 16x20 photos were arranged on the walls of the gallery with another hundred or so 8x10 photographs displayed in a photo album. The exhibit was well received as many people reminisced about the "old days" depicted in these delightful photographs.

It is not known if the thoughts of such an exhibit ever entered Mr. Merritt's mind while he was enjoying this hobby. What we do know is that through his photography this era of life in Roxboro and Person County will always be preserved.

Modern Roxboro

Most of the photographs in this book were taken shortly after the Great Depression. It was during this time that modern Roxboro evolved.

Modern Roxboro was brought about by one man in particular. Of course no one man works completely by himself, and there were a lot of people in the county and the community involved in Roxboro's development. But one man in particular was the leader. His name was J.A "Dee" Long (James Anderson Long). He was born and raised in Person County and served in the Civil War. After the Civil War he came into town to try and make a living because his family had fallen on terribly hard times during the war and was very much in debt. When he came to Roxboro from the Stories Creek area of Person County in 1865 he had acquired quite a bit of land and was a merchant in his own right. He had a vision for Person County and for Roxboro, which brought Roxboro into what we call the modern era. He foresaw the need for a railroad. We were very isolated and had no railroad within twenty or thirty miles in all directions of Roxboro, and the roads in the county were very poor.

Roxboro had been established as the county seat in 1792 when our county was cut off from Caswell County and was named Person County. It had been here a good many years by the time Mr. Long came into town. However, we had not grown or developed to any significant extent. Mr. Long, being a businessman and an entrepreneur, saw needs that had to be filled in order to bring this county more in tune with the times. One of the first things he did that helped to bring us out of isolation was to get the railroad, which was called the L&D (Louisiana and Delta), to run through Person County. When it was connected on both ends from Durham and Lynchburg in 1890 one could say that Roxboro had "arrived." At that point in time we finally had a means for getting our products to market and also for receiving goods that we needed from outside areas. We could go from here to the outside world as individuals and begin to build businesses, enabling us to establish a county that was considered more than just rural.

When the railroad came through, Mr. Long was the first person to have a warehouse ready for the tobacco market where the auctions could take place. When the railroad was joined in August 1890 Mr. Long was ready, and our first tobacco warehouse was opened for the farmers to use here in Roxboro. That meant they did not have to go to Oxford or Henderson or Durham (North Carolina, south of Roxboro) or South Boston (Virginia). Many other people jumped on the bandwagon, so to speak, and other warehouses were opened. Along with them was the establishment of prize houses, which took care of the drying of the tobacco so that it could be stored in the hogsheads and transported to the manufacturers of various tobacco products.

The need for a bank was also recognized. There had been an attempt during the Civil War to have a bank in Roxboro. However, the effort was not successful and it only lasted about three years. It was the timing of that project that was not in its favor—during the Civil War things were very uncertain everywhere. Prior to opening the bank in Roxboro the people had to do their banking in Milton, North Carolina. After the failed effort of establishing a bank here, citizens had to return to Milton for any and all banking needs. However, in 1891 Mr. J.A. "Dee" Long started the People's Bank of Roxboro. Efforts to establish a second bank here around 1893 were short-lived as well. In 1896 it was incorporated into the People's Bank so that there was just one bank here at that time. Banking did expand, however, and in 1913 another bank known as the First National Bank opened. By the 1930s when banking was in such an unstable situation, most of the competitive banks went out of business and the People's Bank was the only one that remained.

Night scene looking north down Main Street.

This is a view of Main Street from across the courthouse lawn. People's Bank can be seen on the corner of Court Street and Main Street.

Shirley King, *left*, and Edith Grey Merritt, *right*, pose on Main Street, Roxboro. This photo was taken just across the street from where Tar Heel Chevrolet used to be.

The Foushee building, located on the east side of Main Street just across from the courthouse.

Unknown child on the courthouse lawn with the People's Bank building at the corner of Main Street and Court Street in the background.

From the east side of Main Street looking north is a view of Long Memorial Methodist Church along with the old Penny Furniture building. This photo was taken from the Roxboro building. The Gulf station was operated by Mr. R.D. Bumpass.

The Great Atlantic & Pacific Tea Company (A&P) was located on Main Street next to the Palace Theater before moving to another location on Abbitt Street.

This building, located on the east side of Main Street, still stands today. For many years the Kaplan family ran a ladies' dress shop in this building. Dances were held on the second floor on weekends. The building eventually became the original site of The Bootery, a locally owned and operated shoe store.

This view is of the west side of Main Street. The Kirby Theater and the Roxboro building can be seen in the background. This photograph was taken in 1949.

This is one of the early buildings on Main Street, known as the Wilburn and Satterfield building. The second floor of this building is where Dr. J.D. Bradsher had his dental office.

Looking west down Court Street, one sees the People's Bank building at the corner of Main Street and Court Street. A barbershop with a Court Street entrance was located in the space in the back of the bank building. Mr. W.D. Merritt's law office was on the second floor. W.D. Merritt was the father of Mr. John W. Merritt.

Citizens National Bank on the east side of Main Street near the corner of Depot Street.

This photo was taken in the late 1940s looking south down Main Street. The Kirby Theater and the Roxboro building can be seen on the west side of Main Street.

Mr. Merritt took this photo from the top of the Roxboro building. The old Tom's Auto Supply building can be seen at the corner of Lamar Street and Court Street. The top of Planters Tobacco Warehouse can be seen in the background.

A night view of Court Street looking toward Main Street. Lighted windows are from the backside of the courthouse.

Roxboro parade, ca. 1952.

Entertainment

Back in the late 1930s and early 1940s the people of Roxboro and Person County did not get in their cars and go to the beach or to Durham or Raleigh for a night out as they do today. They stayed right here and created their own entertainment. One popular spot to go was up to Hager's Mountain. This mountain, as it was called, was out on the Woodsdale Road, and one would have to park down at the base and hike up to the top. People would go up there to have picnics and spend the day or just an hour or so looking out over the county. There are large rocks up there that the people could climb up on, and the view was spectacular.

Another popular place to go for entertainment was the Palace Theater. The history of the Palace goes back many years to the days of silent movies. The picture had no sound and a narrator told the story while someone played an organ or piano for background music. The Kirby brothers, Teague and Cyrus, were the owners. As the story goes, brother Joe was given a partnership when he returned home from World War I, though he never took an active part in the operation.

The theater thrived through the years. Teague was the mastermind, making frequent trips to Charlotte to the distributors to pick up the latest releases. There was a movie for Monday and Tuesday, another for Wednesday and another for Thursday. The "westerns" were shown on Friday and Saturday. Three times a week there was a morning matinée at 10:00 to accommodate people who worked second shift in the local mills. Monday through Friday a movie was shown at 3:00 and two at night, one at 7:00 and one at 9:00. On Saturday there were two movies in the afternoon, one at 2:00 and then one at 4:00. There would be two shows on Saturday evening beginning at 7:00 followed by the second show at 9:00. Wednesday was always jackpot day. This was when the ticket stubs from that day's attendance were placed in a large drum and a child from the audience was chosen to come onstage and draw a winner for one hundred dollars. If no one claimed the jackpot within a week then it grew for the next week. Jackpot day always drew large crowds. Back in the 1930s admission was ten cents for children and twenty-five cents for adults. Occasionally on Saturday there might be a personal appearance of the star of the movie. Then came the midnight shows on Saturday night at 11:30, not exactly family entertainment. Sometimes these shows would be live stage shows. Sunday shows were opposed but eventually were allowed with one show at 3:00 p.m. and one at 8:00 p.m. Sometimes there would be "kiddie" matinées (cartoons) on Saturday when the children were out of school.

Air conditioning was unheard of so the building was cooled with "washed air." This was a system where water flowed over coils and a fan forced the cool air into the building's vents. The stage was used for local functions when needed, such as dance recitals and beauty contests. The office for the operation was on the second floor behind the fan-shaped window on the front. After all of those wonderful years and memories, the Palace Theater closed and the Kirby Theater opened in 1949.

The majorettes of the high school marching band lead the parade down Main Street. The building in the background is the old Tar Heel Chevrolet building, and the one in the foreground is the Royal Café.

A rather large crowd has gathered as a parade moves along Main Street. Roxboro Baptist Church and the dome on top of the People's Bank building can be seen in the background. This parade is moving from the south to the north, unlike today's parades, which move in the opposite direction. This photo was taken ca. 1952. This photo was taken ca. 1952.

The Roxboro High School majorettes lead a parade down Main Street. The Roxboro Hotel on Abbitt Street across from the Person County Courthouse can be seen in the background.

Parade down Main Street.

This building was used for several car dealerships including A.E. Jackson Pontiac and later, Tar Heel Chevrolet. This building is still owned today by the Hall family.

The Carver building is located on the east side of Main Street and is still being used today. The building was built in 1928 by Mr. F.O. Carver.

The steel structure of the Roxboro building while under construction. This photo was taken in late 1948.

The Roxboro building at the corner of Reams Avenue and Main Street.

Mrs. C.C. Critcher, *left*, Mrs. Gordon Hunter, *center*, and Mrs. R.E. Hamlin, right.

These car salesmen compare sales tickets on the corner of Lamar Street and Reams Avenue.

The Roxboro High School marching band leads a parade down Main Street.

The Person County Courthouse was built in the early 1930s to replace the old one.

This is the plane that was used to fly Mr. Merritt over areas of Person County to take aerial photos. This landing strip was located about seven miles north of Roxboro on U.S. 501.

Carolina Broom Works was located on the corner of Depot Street and Foushee Street. This building was built in the mid-1940s.

Person Memorial Hospital is located on Ridge Road. It was built in the early 1950s. Members of Lowell T. Huff Post #2058 planted sixty-six trees at the hospital for the sixty-six Person County soldiers who died in World War II. It was dedicated on September 9, 1950.

Thomas Drugs was locally owned and operated by Mr. Bud Thomas and was located on the corner of Reams Avenue and Madison Boulevard.

Two high school girls pose for the photographer: Edith Grey Merritt, *left*, and Shirley King, right.

This is a view from atop Hager's Mountain. The mountain is located in the Woodsdale Township. When this photograph was taken in the late 1930s Hager's Mountain was a popular spot for Sunday picnics and gatherings.

Another view from atop Hager's Mountain in the late 1930s.

Industry

In 1899 Mr. J.A. "Dee" Long began a textile business in what was known as East Roxboro. He named his business Roxboro Cotton Mill. He had numerous men in town who invested in this business in addition to both the Duke family and the Watts family of Durham. This cotton mill provided employment for a number of people who were not having any success on the farm. Mr. Long was successful with this business, and around 1907 he started another cotton mill in Longhurst, an area of the county originally known as Jalong, named after Mr. J.A. Long. This mill was located about two miles north of the town.

It was after the Longhurst Cotton Mill was established that it was realized that a manufacturing establishment was needed to buy the yarn that was being produced at the cotton mill. About this time Baker Manufacturing Company came to town. The business was located only about one mile from the Longhurst Cotton Mill, and it began buying the yarn from both of the cotton mills here in Roxboro. Baker's stayed in business here until about 1926, at which time it was acquired by a company called Collins and Aikman. Collins and Aikman continued to make cotton velvet.

The little village in which the workers lived and where the executives of the plant lived was named Ca-vel. This stood for Collins and Aikman, "Ca," and it was hyphenated with the "vel" of Collins and Aikman Velvet. The hyphen has since been removed and it is currently known as Cavel.

The Longhurst Cotton Mill, the Roxboro Cotton Mill and the Collins and Aikman businesses all had what were called mill villages. These mill villages were in effect self-contained villages, meaning that they had their own grocery store, their own school and their own churches. They even had their own entertainment in the form of ball teams for both men and women. From these ball teams have emerged some very outstanding athletes, most notably one named Enos Slaughter who went on to become a member of the Baseball Hall of Fame.

This building, located on Depot Street, was used as a Ford Motor Company agency and was operated by Arch Jones and Joe Kirby. This building stills stands today.

Gold Seal Dairy with delivery trucks and drivers lined up.

This dairy barn, which still stands today, is on Henry Street. This was known as the Foushee Dairy. The cows were owned by Mr. R.D. Bumpass.

A large assortment of dairy treats was sold at the Gold Seal Dairy.

Another view of the Gold Seal Dairy.

Inside Gold Seal Dairy.

The employees of Gold Seal Dairy.

This is a photo of the ribbon-cutting ceremony held at Thomas & Oakley Drugstore. Curtis Oakley is standing on the right and Phil Thomas can be seen on the left. The girl standing on the far left is Eva Oakley, the daughter of Curtis Oakley.

The crowd gathers outside, waiting for the grand opening of Thomas & Oakley Drugstore.

Another scene outside T&O Drugstore.

This is another view of opening night. Notice Mrs. Jean Newell standing on the balcony next to the Shank's Grill sign. She and her husband, Mr. Henry Newell Sr., lived in this apartment for a while during the late 1940s.

The newly completed Kirby Theater on Main Street was operated by the O.T. Kirby family. Shanks's Grill was located next door and was operated by Shank Bumpass.

Another view of the Kirby Theater taken shortly before its grand opening in 1949.

Crowds gather outside the Kirby Theater on opening night for the first showing of *The Stratton Story* starring James Stewart and June Allison.

The projection room at the Kirby Theater was operated by Graham Roberson. Mr. Roberson was also the projectionist at the Palace Theater.

This photo, showing both the stage and decorative murals, was taken inside the Kirby Theater on August 31, 1949, the day of the grand opening.

This is a wooden carving that stood in the lobby of the Kirby Theater.

Person County's farmers looking over the new Case tractors.

Mr. Bill Winstead ran this tractor dealership in the 1950s. It was located on the Durham Road just past the J.A. Humphries store.

Another photo of the Case tractor dealership.

The latest in Case tractors.

The man in the suit is Mr. Bill Winstead, the owner of the tractor dealership.

Inside Mr. Bill Winstead's tractor dealership.

This would have been a typical scene here in Person County back in the 1950s. Notice the slide being pulled by the mules.

This is one of many tobacco barns in Person County. The woodpile stacked up in front of the barn was used to cure the tobacco. Workers would have to tend these barns twenty-four hours a day to keep the heat at just the right temperature.

Tobacco barns were part of the landscape all over Person County.

At the barn a mule waits for the slides to be unloaded.

A typical Person County farm scene from the 1950s.

Growing tobacco in the fields was only part of taking care of the crop. Once the tobacco had been pulled it had to be strung on sticks and put in the barns to dry. All of this had to be done by hand. The barns had to be fired by hand and the temperature maintained day and night for about a week.

Piles of tobacco waiting to be sold at Hyco Warehouse.

More tobacco on the warehouse floor awaiting auction.

Tobacco is being prepared for auction in Hyco Warehouse. At the time of this photo Hyco Warehouse was located on Depot Street not far from Main Street.

An auction of tobacco in one of several warehouses in Roxboro.

Tobacco is being brought into one of the local warehouses for auction. Families worked at the barns to prepare the tobacco leaves for curing. The tobacco was brought out of the fields in slides pulled by mules.

Olive Hill School was located about four miles west of Roxboro on N.C. 57. Students in grades one through six attended this school and then transferred to Roxboro High School. Olive Hill School was demolished in 1974.

Another photograph of the Olive Hill School.

Hurdle Mills School, which no longer stands.

Allensville School, built by George W. Kane.

Longhurst School was an elementary school that was used to accommodate children of families in the Longhurst Mill village. It was built by Mr. J.A. "Dee" Long and was located about two miles north of Roxboro on U.S. 501.

Bethel Hill School served as a place of education for children in the northern part of the county from grades one through six.

Roxboro High School was located on Morgan Street. As the population grew, extra space was needed and the school was expanded on each end.

This is the Roxboro High School gym. It still stands today and is used for sporting events. It was built by George W. Kane.

Central School was located on Gordon Street between Main Street and Lamar Street. Grades one through six attended this school. This school was once the high school before the new school was built on Morgan Street. It was built in 1908, the same year that the Roxboro Hotel was built.

Central School.

A fourth-grade class at Central School and their teacher, Miss Inda Collins.

A basketball game at the old Roxboro High School located on Morgan Street.

A Roxboro High School basketball game.

Brooksdale United Methodist Church.

Long Memorial Methodist Church is located on Main Street next to the business district. The J.A. Long family had much to do with building this church, so it was named Edgar Long Memorial. The house next to it was occupied by the pastor. It was built ca. 1918.

High school club photo taken just before a performance at Long Memorial Methodist Church.

Longhurst Methodist Church.

Grace Methodist Church was located in east Roxboro for the purpose of serving families who lived and worked at the Roxboro Cotton Mill.

Roxboro Presbyterian Church, located at the corner of Lamar Street and Oak Street.

Another view of Roxboro Presbyterian Church, first known as Mebane Memorial.

View from Madison Boulevard of Roxboro Presbyterian Church.

The Roxboro Baptist Church and Educational Building is located at the corner of Main Street and Academy Street. This building replaced a small wooden structure that was situated at the same location in the 1950s. The left section of this building was built in the early 1940s.

Intersection of Ivy Street and Madison Boulevard during the early 1950s.

The center of this photo is where the Person County Health Department is now located in the former Wal-Mart building. Madison Boulevard is located just below the center, which looks like the main road. Lamar Street is just underneath it. Notice there is more traffic on Lamar Street than on Madison Boulevard, which is the busiest street in Roxboro today.

Another view of Madison Boulevard and the uptown district of Roxboro.

The Old Durham Road merging with the Durham Road.

U.S. 501 North leading out of Roxboro with the Collins and Aikman plant in the background.

Aerial view of Madison Boulevard with the business district in the background.

The house in the background is where the Homestead Florist is located today. Hump's Grill was in the building that is now occupied by Henry's Quick Stop.

This is the J.A. Humphries grocery store, located on the Durham Road just beyond the intersection with the Hurdle Mills Road. The left side was a sandwich shop operated most of the time by family members.

These girls pose in bathing suits for an upcoming beauty pageant at the Hill Top Swimming Pool. These photos were made to be used to advertise the event.

About nine miles down the Virgilina Road in the Olive Branch Community was another public swimming pool operated by Pots Gentry. It was known as the Triple Springs Swimming Pool. It wasn't as large as Hill Top but it was always busy. The Gentry family operated a grocery store, and snacks and drinks were available. There were three springs located nearby that were used to fill the pool. It was these three springs that gave Triple Springs its name.

Triple Springs Swimming Pool, early 1950s.

Another view of the Triple Springs Swimming Pool.

Triple Springs Swimming Pool.

Marty's Grill was located on Madison Boulevard at the corner of what is now Morehead Street. At the time this photo was taken Morehead Street had not yet been built.

The Rocket Grill was one of the early businesses on Madison Boulevard. This building is no longer standing. The Rocket Grill and Marty's Grill were both owned by Mr. Jack Martin.

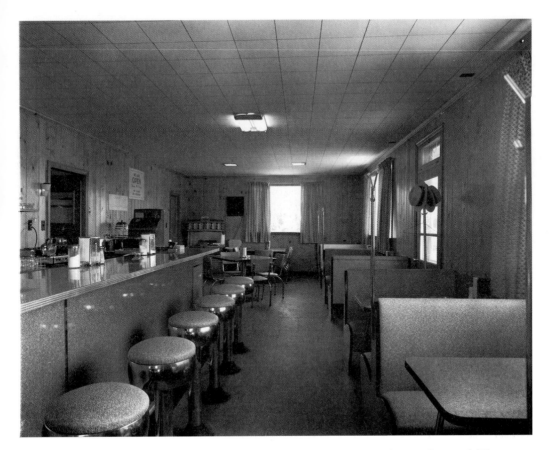

The Rocket Grill was a restaurant where one could get a complete or short-order meal. There were several owners after Mr. Martin. Finally, the property was sold and demolished to make room for new businesses on Madison Boulevard.

Eric's Drive-In on the corner of Leasburg Road and Morgan Street. This was a great place for young people to enjoy good food and dancing.

Another view of Eric's Drive-In, which was operated by Mr. Eric Garrett.

This is a crowd at the VFW/Person County Fair, which was held in October of each year. This location is across the railroad tracks on the Virgilina Road, also known as N.C. 49.

Another view of the Person County Fair.

Crowd at the Person County/VFW Fair with the rides in the background.

Person County Fair, early 1940s.

A group of ladies in costume for a meeting of the Research Club, May 25, 1952.

The Roxboro depot was a very active place at one time. Norfolk & Western trains passed through several times a day going between Durham, North Carolina, and Lynchburg, Virginia. There were passenger and mail trains that came through at 12:00, 3:00 and 6:00 p.m. The freight train would come in at 8:00 a.m. bringing in freight for the uptown businesses. It would also bring coal, lumber and cotton for the cotton mills. Frequently, one would see a hobo hiding in a boxcar riding the rails. This was against the law so the trains were searched, but the hobos would jump off before the train reached the station.

A Norfolk & Western freight train derailed at Longhurst about two miles north of Roxboro after a heavy rain washed out the track. Crowds gathered to watch the removal of the wreckage. These photos were taken in the early 1950s.

Another view of the train derailment at Longhurst.

Longhurst train derailment.

Longhurst train derailment.

Train wreck.

This is a photograph of Baker Manufacturing Company located just north of the Longhurst Cotton Mill. They used the yarn from the two cotton mills here to produce cotton velvet. Baker's stayed in business here until about 1926, when they were bought by Collins and Aikman.

These are looms located in the weave room at the Collins and Aikman plant. These looms held the fabric that was used in the furniture industry and also used to cover paint rollers. These beams of cloth were about six feet in length.

Pictured here is another view of the looms that were in the weave room at the Collins and Aikman plant.

This is a Jacquard loom that was used to make a fabric that was used in the upholstery business. Upon looking closely at this photograph, one is able to see the floral design that was put onto the fabric with this machine. This is an original machine that was made by the Collins and Aikman plant. The cords up on top of the machine were called lingo cords. At one time there were about fifty of these machines in the Collins and Aikman plant.

After the cloth was removed from the loom it would go to this machine, which was located in the finishing department. The duct work up on top was used to remove any lint that was on the cloth and also to give the cloth its final finish. Much of this cloth was used to make paint rollers.

This is one of several dye kettles that was used at the Collins and Aikman plant. Any cloth that needed to be dyed was dyed in these kettles.

Longhurst Cotton Mill, built ca. 1907 by Mr. J.A. "Dee" Long. The Longhurst mill spun a yarn that was used by the Baker Manufacturing Company located about one mile up the road from the Longhurst plant. Baker Manufacturing became Collins and Aikman ca. 1926.

Another view of the Longhurst Cotton Mill.

This photo of W.W. Morrell, manager of both Roxboro Cotton Mill and Longhurst Cotton Mill, was made in 1958.

Lester Morrell became manager of both the Roxboro Cotton Mill and the Longhurst mill after his father, W.W. Morrell, retired.

Cotton is being unloaded from the railcars at the Longhurst plant. These bales were weighed first and then graded. The next stop for the cotton after being graded was for it to be tested in the lab.

This is the lab where the cotton was checked to make sure it was of the highest quality.

This is what was called the opening room at the Longhurst plant. The cotton on the floor has already been to the lab and is ready to be blended.

This is the card room where the cotton would be cleaned.

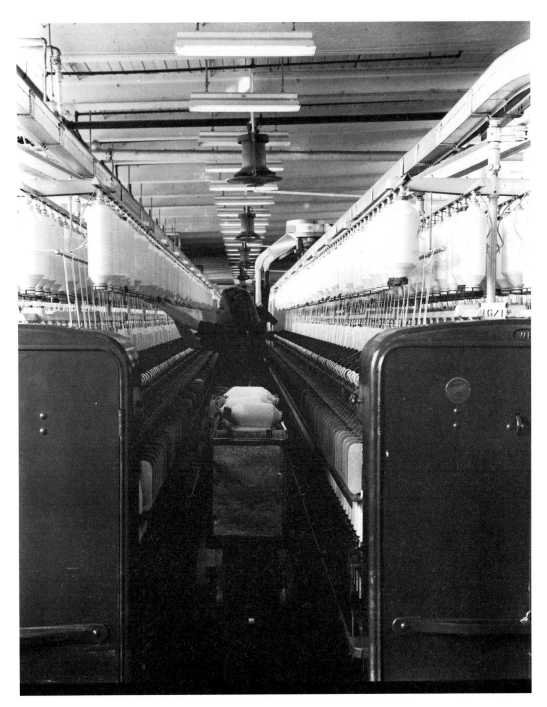

The bobbins on top were called roving bobbins. The machine on top in the background is a vacuum that would run around on a track system to vacuum up any lint that would come off of the cotton. Lint was a big problem at both the Longhurst Cotton Mill and the Roxboro Cotton Mill.

The bobbins on the bottom were called spinning bobbins. The yarn on these bobbins was then made into the twisters, which you see up on top. Notice the vacuum up on top to remove any lint that needed to be cleaned.

Here is another view of the spinning bobbins on the bottom being made into twisters.

This was called the winding room. It was here that the yarn could either be put onto cones or tubes to be made ready for shipping.

Rolls of twisters waiting to be processed.

All the machines at both cotton mills in Roxboro had to be maintained daily to make sure they were in top running condition.

The spooler bobbins are on the bottom and the twisters are on top.

Here is a good view of the vacuum system that ran up on top of these spinning frames to keep the lint problem under control.

Another view of the spinning frames.

Mr. Otis Stephens is seen here checking out the twisters at the Longhurst mill. Mr. Stephens was an overseer at the Longhurst Cotton Mill from 1943 until 1967. He held the same position at the Roxboro Cotton Mill from 1967 until 1991.

Roving frames.

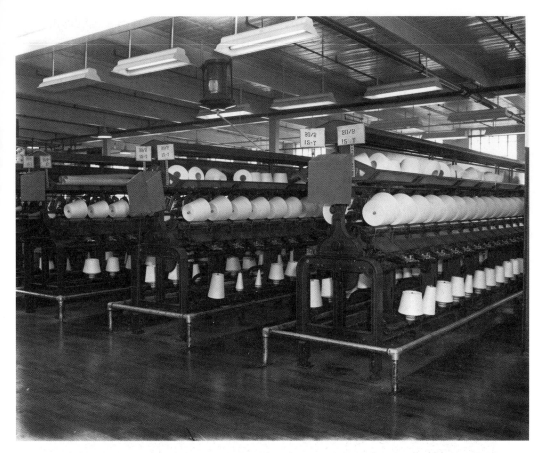

Pictured here are the winders at the Longhurst Cotton Mill. These winders held the finished yarn.

Mr. Miller checking to make sure the machines are running properly. Mr. Miller looked after not only repairing the machines at both cotton mills, but he also did repairs on the houses that were located in the mill village.

This is the winding room at the Roxboro plant. The man in the photo is Mr. Artie Snead, who was an overseer at the Roxboro plant.

Many employees of the Roxboro Cotton Mill lived in these houses in east Roxboro. Most of these houses were owned by the cotton mill and were then rented to the employees.

The Roxboro Cotton Mill was located in east Roxboro. Mr. J.A. "Dee" Long, the founder of modern Roxboro, built this textile business in 1899. This building was completely renovated in 2006 and it is now the location of the Roxboro Charter School.

Another view of the parade from the late 1940s.

This is a photograph of a parade down Main Street Roxboro taken in the late 1940s. The Pioneer Warehouse was demolished to make room for the Roxboro building, which was built in the early 1950s. The bowling alley in the background was located in what is now the Kirby building.

Mr. Merritt made his one and only trip to Myrtle Beach, South Carolina, in the early 1950s and took this photo of the Myrtle Beach Pavilion. This pavilion was built in 1948 and was demolished in late 2006.

Visit us at
www.historypress.net